Bibliographic information published by the German National Library:

The German National Library lists this publication in the National Bibliography; detailed bibliographic data are available on the Internet at http://dnb.dnb.de .

Imprint:

Copyright © 2011 GRIN Verlag, Open Publishing GmbH
Print and binding: Books on Demand GmbH, Norderstedt Germany
ISBN: 9783668473188

This book at GRIN:

http://www.grin.com/en/e-book/367040/spying-software-development-in-google-android

Fissha SeyoumTeshome

Spying Software Development in Google Android

GRIN Publishing

GRIN - Your knowledge has value

Since its foundation in 1998, GRIN has specialized in publishing academic texts by students, college teachers and other academics as e-book and printed book. The website www.grin.com is an ideal platform for presenting term papers, final papers, scientific essays, dissertations and specialist books.

Visit us on the internet:

http://www.grin.com/

http://www.facebook.com/grincom

http://www.twitter.com/grin_com

CONTENTS

1 Introduction

In today's world the use of mobile phones has become a common custom and this has resulted in a great demand of a mobile phone applications. Among the millions of mobile phone applications one is spying software. Spying software is software mainly developed to track the location of mobile phone, reading Short Message Service (SMS), Email, and Call Logs secretly and making a spy call. The existence of spying software is controversial. First, there are millions of phone users who are concerned about their privacy. On the other hand there are millions who use spying software application for good or bad reasons. Second, there are many companies who develop such applications, while there are others who develop the security against such applications.

The purpose of this project is to study the concept behind developing spying software for a mobile phone. The goal of this project is to develop a location tracker application for a Google Android phone. However, the tracker application should take into consideration Google Android mobile phones equipped with a Global Positioning System (GPS) or those which do not have it or those who have it deactivated. In the absence of a GPS for any reason, the use of Cell Identification (Cell-ID) will come into use.

The scope of this project is limited to tracking the location of Google Android phones. One reason is that adding other features such as a call interceptor or SMS coping would make the application suspicious. Another reason is that Google does not support the development of spying software because Google wants to keep the privacy of Google Android phone users.

2 Spying Software Market

2.1 Mobile Spying Software

Mobile spying software is software that can be installed on a target phone for a number of purposes. Services provided by such software based on a phone call include Secretly Record Calls and Room Monitoring. **Secretly Record Calls** records all calls made from or to specific numbers on the mobile phone. The secretly recorded calls are then uploaded to an online account. **Room Monitoring** (**Spy Call**) remotely records all conversations and sounds within a certain proximity of the target's mobile phone. This is normally achieved by activating the auto-answer setting of the target's mobile phone, which will then trigger the recording to start. Once complete, the recording will be uploaded to an online account. [1; 2]

Other services of such software which are monitored by the server of the spying software's owner include GPS Tracking, Secretly Read Text Messages, Call History, Browser History Bookmarks, Contact Details, and Secretly Retrieve Pictures &Videos. **GPS Tracking** records GPS coordinates of the target's cell, and uploads the data to an online account. **Secretly Read Text Messages** secretly reads all text messages that are sent and received from the target's mobile phone. **Call History** records all incoming and outgoing call data and uploads it to an online account. **Browser History** views the history of the phone's web browser. **Bookmarks** views all the web bookmarks stored. **Contact Details** views contact details that are stored on the phone. **Secretly Retrieve Pictures &Videos** secretly retrieves and views photos and videos that are on the target's mobile phone. [1; 2]

Furthermore, there are services such as SIM Change Notification and Location Information which are based on the SMS service and phone state change. **SIM Change Notification** sends an SMS that contains the details of the new SIM card including the new number of the target's mobile phone to the specified number. **Location Information** obtains the current location of the target's mobile phone. This is done by sending secretly a text message to the target's phone. [1; 3]

The features mentioned above are found almost in all mobile spying software. Different venders have different policies about how to use their software. [1; 2]

Mobile spying software as a term is a general name given for all spying software developed for different phone models. Different models mean mobile phone devices running different mobile phone Operating Systems (OSes). The most commonly used mobile spying software are discussed in the following.

Flexiyspy is spying software mainly developed for Symbian, Blackberry, and Windows mobile OSes. It has different versions: Pro-X, Pro, Light, Bug, Record, and Shield. The main features and summarized in table 1. [3]

Table 1. FlexiySpy different versions and their features. [3]

Features	Flexispy's Different versions					
	Pro-X	Pro	Light	Bug	Record	Shiled
Remote listening	yes	yes		yes	yes	
Control phone by SMS	yes	yes	yes	yes	yes	
SMS and email logging	yes	yes	yes			
Call history logging	yes	yes	yes			
Location Tracking	yes	yes	yes			
Call Interception	yes				yes	
Gps Tracking	yes					
Shiled						yes
Black and White list						yes
Listen to recorded conversation					yes	
GPRS capability required	yes	yes	yes			
SIM change notification	yes	yes		yes		
Blackberry messenger	yes					

This product supports a number of OSes. The supported OSes by the different FlexiySpy versions are summarized in table 2. [3]

Table 2. FlexiySpy different versions and supported OSes. [3]

Supported OSes	Flexiyspy different versions					
	Pro-X	Pro	Light	Bug	Record	Shield
Symbian	yes	yes	yes	yes		yes
Blackberry	yes	yes	yes	yes		
Windows	yes	yes	yes	yes	yes	

FlexiySpy also provides web service for customers. The web services of FlexiySpy have the following important features:

- The web account is protected using Secure Socket Layer (SSL) technology.
- Using the web account a customer can view all the location, SMS, email and phone activity in an easy format.
- A customer can carry out searches for key words in email or SMS, phone numbers, contact names over selectable periods in time.
- A customer can generate reports to download in PDF, CSV or RTF format for evidence or backup. [3]

Mobile spy is spying software that also has a number features but while using this software the target phone data will be recorded and uploaded on a web server. Many of the services of this software are monitored by the company's server. In other words, every event of the target phone will be uploaded to the company's server database. The services include Call Log, SMS Log, Contacts, E-Mail Log, Calendar Events, URL Log and Photo & Video Log. **Call Log** means that each incoming and outgoing number is logged along with duration and time stamp. **SMS Log** means that every text message is logged. The logging will have text data even if the phone's logs are deleted. In **Contacts** every contact on the phone is logged. **E-Mail Log** records all inbound and outbound email activity from the primary email account. **Calendar Events** logs every calendar event in which date, time, and locations are recorded. **URL Log** logs all URL website addresses visited using the phone's browser. **Photo** and **Video Log** records all photos and videos taken by the phone. [1]

Other features such as GPS Locations and Cell ID Locations are based on the same principle. The difference is they are used to trace the location of the target phone. In **GPS Locations Log** GPS positions are uploaded every 30 minutes with a link to a map. In **Cell ID Locations** ID information on all cell towers that the device enters is recorded. [1]

In order to access all recorded activities the customer should log into an online account created at the purchasing time. This software is mainly developed for Symbian, Blackberry, Android, Widows, and iPhone mobile OSes. [1]

Neo call provides also unsusceptible mobile spying with a number of features as well. Many of Neo call software services are based on the SMS service to the PreDefinedNumber (PDN). These includes Multi Master control number, Status Report by SMS, Remote Controlling and Configuration by SMS, International and Country locked software version, Delivery by Download/SMS/Email/Memory card, Password Protected Secret commands, Reboot (phone / software) remotely by SMS, and Incoming/ outcoming SMS Forwarding. [4]

With the **Multi Master Control Number** a customer can set up a PDN and use it to control one or more Neo call devices. **Status Report by SMS** means that the customer can get real-time status directly to the PDN with an easy command request. **Remote Controlling and Configuration** by **SMS** the customer can use NeoCall all over the world if not bought country-locked version. **Delivery by Download/SMS/Email/Memory card** the customer can get the file directly from a web link sent using an SMS, email or by a memory card with a setup file. **Password Protected Secret Commands** means that the customer can send commands by SMS with a specific password. **Reboot (phone / software) Remotely** by **SMS** with this the customer can reboot both the phone and software after changing setup by sending specific SMS. **Incoming/Outcoming SMS Forwarding** means that the customer can receive every SMS sent or received to the PDN in real-time. [4]

Other services are based on the SMS service, phone state change and phone calls. These include Call List by SMS, Sim Change and Power-On Notification, Delivery SMS and Call List by Bluetooth/Email, Environment Listening, and Call Intercept (Listen conversation). **Call List** by **SMS** means that the customer can get all missed/sent/incoming call list by SMS. With the **Sim Change** and **Power-On Notification** the customer can get informed when a new SIM is inserted on the target phone. **Delivery SMS and Call List** by **Bluetooth/Email** means that the customer can receive SMS contents or Log directly to the mailbox. **Environment Listening** means that after making a spy call the customer can here the surrounding environment. **Call Intercept** (**Listen conversation**) with this the customer can hear the conversation between two people after calling target phone with a hidden conference call. [4]

Finally, location-based services such as Cell Base Location and GPS Information are provided by this software. **Cell Base Location** means that data about the cell where the target phone is connected to can be retrieved and this helps to get the geo location of the target. **GPS Information** with this target position can be retrieved using satellite data (i.e. Longitude and Latitude) and a high precision map can be obtained. [4]

Neocall has different versions. The versions are different since not all have similar features. These are Basic, Standard, Pro and Full package while Full package as the name implies having all features described above. Further Neocall has a special version called Windows mobile with the least number of features from those listed above. Neocall has the list number of supported OSes. These are BlackBerry and Symbian phones. [4]

NokiaSpyPhones can secretly record events that have happened on the target phone and deliver the information to a mobile phone via SMS or to a secure Internet account, where this information can be viewed from an Internet-enabled computer or mobile phone. They have features such as Call Interception, Call History Recording, Environment Listening, SMS Recording, Email Recording, GPS Tracking, Cell ID Location, SIM Change Notification, and Web Support (i.e. viewing all records of the target phone via a web account and downloading the information retrieved). This software has different packages by considering a number of features supported. Supported OSes include Symbian, Blackberry, and iPhone. [5]

E-stealth, or with a special product named **Ultimate Mobile Phone Spy**, runs on mobile phones for similar spying purposes. This software is mainly dependent on Bluetooth technology, in other words, the target phone Bluetooth should be used. Features include performing blue bug attack, initiating voice call, retrieving numbers, setting call forward, and retrieving SMS. This software was mainly developed for Symbian phones but now the software supports iPhone and Blackberry. [6]

2.2 Antispy Software

Mobile spying software is considered to be spyware or even a Trojan by antivirus and antispy software developer companies. Antispy Software developers have declared such software as spyware, even if spying software developers claim that a typical application for such tools is to keep track of one's spouse, or to monitor one's children, or just to keep track of one's own phone in use. Antispy software developers share these reasons to declare mobile spying software as spyware. First, if victim have a full featured spy application installed on their phone, they have no privacy, and the one controlling the software has access to all of the information that the phone has. Second, even if the spy software vendors state that their software should be used only in accordance with local laws, the vendors take no responsibility for how their software is actually used, and in many countries such monitoring is viewed as gross violation of personal privacy and can end up in a jail sentence. Also these tools have darker uses such as industrial espionage, identity theft, or stalking. [7] The main types of antispy software are discussed below.

F-Secure Mobile Security is developed by F-Secure to protect mobile phones against mobile spying software. The key features include complete security solution for smart phones with automatic updates, safeguarding one's personal and confidential data, identifying dangerous websites and protecting one's identity online, locating a lost or stolen phone, or the person holding it, and protecting against viruses and other malware. This software provides support for Symbian, iPhone and Blackberry currently. [8]

Kaspersky Mobile Security 9 provides antispy defense with Internet threat protection to ensure the safe use of mobile phones. The software aims at guarding personal data in situations where a phone is lost or stolen, or is targeted while surfing the Internet. Important features include disabling stolen phone even if the SIM card has been replaced, providing Google Maps coordinates, blocking unwanted calls and texts from specified or unknown numbers, providing real-time virus scanning and advanced firewall for all time protection, and hiding designated contacts, calls, and

SMS texts with privacy mode. This software is mainly developed for Symbian, iPhone and Windows. [9]

BullGuard Mobile Anti Virus provides a solution that protects mobile phones from malicious programs that target mobile platforms, including Viruses, Worms and Trojans which have speared to mobile phones. The AntiVirus software can scan all incoming traffic such as SMS and MMS messages, Bluetooth, Emails and downloads of malicious programs. If the software has been set to auto-scan, it will detect spying software. This Software is developed only for Symbian and Windows Mobile at the moment. [10]

3   Software Development in Android

3.1   Google Android

"Android is a software stack for mobile devices that includes an operating system, middleware and key applications. The Android Software Development Kit (SDK) provides the tools and application Programming Interfaces (APIs) necessary to begin developing applications on the Android platform using the Java programming language." [11; 22; 25]

Android is open-source OS that was released by Google with the Open Handset Alliance (OHA) in November 2007, and this has decreased the barrier to application development. [12; 28]

"The OHA is a group of 65 technology and mobile companies who have come together to accelerate innovation in mobile and offer consumers a richer, less expensive, and better mobile experience. Together we have developed Android™, the first complete, open, and free mobile platform. We are committed to commercially deploy handsets and services using the Android Platform." [13]

T-Mobile G1 was the first Android mobile handset which was released in the United States in October 2008 and in the United Kingdom in November 2008. Google Android is designed to support both touch-screen phones and those without a touch-screen. The Android timeline is shown in figure 1, showing the most important Android-related events through the years. The timeline extends from 2001 until December 1010 while most of the events have happened between the years 2007 and 2010. From the timeline it is possible to see that more and more mobile phone software and device manufacturing companies are getting interested to use Android. The timeline also shows that more members have joined the OHA. [13; 14]

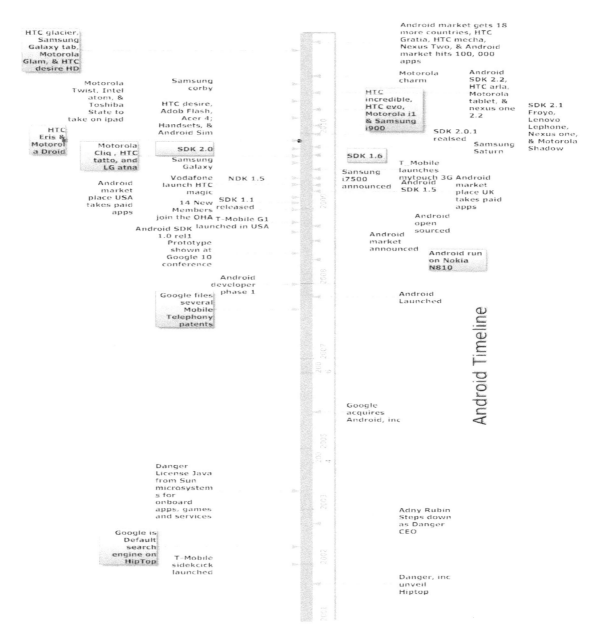

Figure 1: Android timeline from September 2001 to December 2010. Modified from Android Academy. [29]

When discussing an Android OS, it is important to see the underlying architecture, since the handset runs a Linux 2.6 kernel in which all applications run in their own virtual machine. The Linux kernel handles all core systems and acts as a hardware abstraction layer. It is designed to act as an abstraction layer between the physical hardware of the handset and the Android software stack. [20, 23-25] The major components of the Android OS are demonstrated in figure 2.

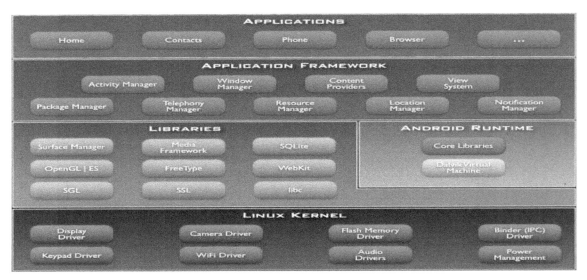

Figure 2: The major components of the Android OS. Reprinted from Android Developers. [30]

As seen from figure 2 above the architecture include different components from Applications layer which is the top layer to Linux kernel. The components are described briefly below.

Applications are a set of core applications including an email client, SMS program, calendar, maps, browser, contacts, and others. These are written using the Java programming language. [11; 20; 26]

Application Framework allows developers to take advantage of the device hardware, access location information, run background services, set alarms, add notifications to the status bar, and much more. Further, developers can have access to the same framework APIs used by the core applications. This component of the architecture is designed to reuse components; in other words, any application can publish its capabilities and any other application may then make use of them. Many of the sub-components of the Application Framework are discussed below.

Activity Manager and Windows Manager are responsible for managing activity and managing the view respectively. **Activity Manager** manages activities as an activity stack. Every activity has four states: Running (active), Paused, Stopped, and Killed. **Window Manager** manages views by implementing ViewManager. The ViewManager has three public abstract methods to be implemented: addView (View view,

ViewGroup.LayoutParamsparams),removeView (View view), and updateViewLayout (View view, and ViewGroup.LayoutParamsparams).

Further, Content providers, Resource Manager and Notification Manager have their own roles. **Content providers** are the only way to share data across applications since there is no common storage area that all Android packages can access. Content provider store and retrieve data in order to make it accessible by all applications. **Resource Manager** provide access to non-code resources such as localized strings, graphics, and layout files. **Notification Manager** enables all applications to display user prompts in the status bar. [11; 20; 27]

Libraries are a set of C/C++ libraries used by various components of the Android system. Through application Frameworks developers are able to access these capabilities. [23] Some parts of the libraries are explained below.

The graphics and bitmap libraries include Scalable Graphics Library (SGL), OpenGL|ES, and FreeType. **SGL** is the underlying 2D graphics engine used by Android. OpenGL|ES contains 3D libraries which are implemented based on OpenGL ES 1.0 APIs. **FreeType** is part of the Android library used for bitmap and vector font rendering. [11; 20]

Libraries such as System C library (libc) and Media Framework are huge in size and used by the Android system. **C library** is a standard C system library specifically for embedded Linux-based devices. **Media Framework** is a collection of libraries which support playback and recording of many popular audio and video formats. [11; 20]

Finally, WebKit and SQLite are powerful engines used by the Android system. **WebKit** is a web browser engine which powers both the Android browser and an embeddable web view. SQLite is a lightweight Structured Query Language (SQL) database engine available to all applications. [11; 20]

Android Runtime consists of the Core Libraries and the Dalvik Virtual Machine (DalvikVM). **Core Libraries** contains a set of core libraries that provide most of the functionality available in the core libraries of the Java programming language.

DalvikVM enables each Android application to run in a separate process, with its own instance of the DalvikVM. The DalvikVM is optimized for mobile devices. Multiple instances of DalvikVm can run concurrently since the DalvikVM executes file to Dalvikexcutable format (.dex) which results in small memory footprints. It relies on the Linux kernel for underlying functionalities such as threading and low-level memory management. [11; 20; 24]

Linux Kernel is based on Linux version 2.6 which is the bases for Android software stack. It provides core system services such as security, memory management, process management, network stack, and driver model. It is also an abstraction layer between the hardware of the handsets and the rest of the software stack. [11; 20]

Further, Google Android Provides a number of features which are responsible for the competiveness of the OS. The current general features are summarized in table 3.

Table 3: Google Android Features. [11]

Feature	Description
Application Framework	Application framework enabling reuse and replacement of components
Dalvik Virtual machine	Dalvik virtual machine optimized for mobile devices
Browser	Integrated browser based on the open source WebKit engine
Graphics	Optimized graphics powered by a custom 2D graphics library; 3D graphics based on the OpenGL ES 1.0 specification (hardware acceleration optional)
Data Storage	SQLite for structured data storage
Media	Media support for common audio, video, and still image formats (MPEG4, H.264, MP3, AAC, AMR, JPG, PNG, GIF)
Connectivity	GSM Telephony, Bluetooth, EDGE, 3G, and WiFi (hardware dependent).
Development environment	Rich development environment including a device emulator, tools for debugging, memory and performance profiling, and a plugin for the Eclipse IDE
Android Market	Android Market is an online software store developed by Google for Android devices. It is used to browse and download applications published by third-party developers.
Others	Messaging, Camera, GPS, compass, and accelerometer (hardware dependent).

Even though table 3 did not include Android Just-In-Time Compiler (JIT), it is important to trace its impact. With Dalvik JIT at Android 2.2 the performance has a speed of two to five times faster for CPU-heavy code over Android 2.1. [31]

3.2   Developing in Android Environment

Many mobile phone application developers have proved that they can develop any kind of application using Android, which was possible also in other competitive OSes. This approval of developers is backed up with the fact that Android has a simple and powerful SDK, no licensing fees, excellent documentation, and a thriving developer community. In addition to these reasons mentioned, Android is backed by 65 members of OHA who are working hard for the success. Furthermore, with excellent features, which are shown in table 3, Android has remarkable market growth.

Figure 3 shows that Android is liked by third-party developers and they are developing several free applications. [13; 21]

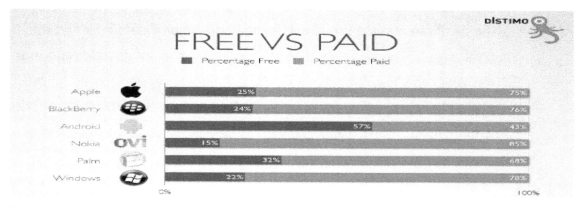

Figure 3: Free VS Paid Applications comparison. Reprinted from Read Write Web. [32]

As figure 3 illustrates, Google Android market has the highest percentage of free applications compared to other application stores. This can be considered a good sign for Google Android application users but bad news for developers and further for end-users.

The bad news for developers is that the Android marketplace takes paid applications currently for a number of countries, namely Argentina, Australia, Austria, Belgium,

Brazil, Canada, Denmark, Finland, France, Germany, Hong Kong, Ireland, Israel, Italy, Japan, Mexico, Netherlands, New Zealand, Norway, Portugal, Russia, Singapore, South Korea, Spain, Sweden, Switzerland, Taiwan, United Kingdom, and United States. This implies that other developers located other than the Countries listed above cannot sell applications and make money. Another issue for developers is the billing system in which Google has limited the billing system only by using Google Checkout. According to a recent survey result, many developers feel that Google Checkout is responsible for the low download volume of their applications. Many are convinced that if Google could use other billing systems such as a carrier billing system, they would have made more money than now. [15; 16; 17; 18]

There are also bad news for end-users. First, currently Android phone users can buy paid applications only if they are located in the following countries: Argentina, Australia, Austria, Belgium, Brazil, Canada, Czech Republic, Denmark, Finland , France, Germany, Hong Kong, India, Ireland, Israel, Italy, Japan, Mexico, Netherlands, New Zealand, Norway, Poland, Portugal, Russia, Singapore, Spain, Sweden Switzerland, Taiwan, United Kingdom, and United States. Second, there is no certificate authority when signing applications since it is completely allowed to use self-signed certificates. The certificate private key is held by the application's developer and the developer can digital sign it. This self-signed certification system is not good for end-users who would download and install applications from Android Marketplace as if the software had quality. In other words, this might also lead the developers not to consider the quality of the software they developed and to be less motivated to put further work on the software they developed. [15; 16; 17; 18; 19]

4 Developing a Tracker Application in Android Environment

4.1 Software Requirement Specifications

The following section will discuss the product requirement specifications named Soft2050 briefly.

4.1.1 Product

The product is Tracking Software for a mobile phone named "Soft2050". The software is to be developed for Android mobile phone users who wish to track their mobile phone. "Soft2050" Android application involved Android User interfaces, Location Based Services, BroadcastReceiver, Notifications and Messaging.

Product Functions

The software provides the user with two options in order to track the target phone. These are either using Cell-ID or by GPS. Only the user of the application or someone who installed it will know the secret SMS to be sent to the target phone when there is the need to track the target phone.

The software will respond according to the secret SMS type. If the SMS body contains the correct string that matches that of the location by Cell-ID service, the application sends back the location of the phone to be tracked. If the SMS body contains the correct string that matches that of the GPS service provided that the use of the GPS is enabled by the user of the target phone, the application sends back the location of the target phone. If the user selected GPS and forgot to enable the GPS on the phone, the application should at least send back the last known location of the device. In both services the location information will include a link to the map, longitude and latitude, street address, post code, and region name of the target phone location.

User Characteristics

User activities are illustrated in figure 4 which shows the Usecase diagram of the application.

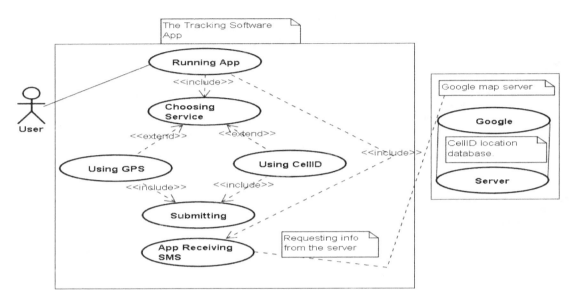

Figure 4: The UseCase diagram for the tracking software application.

In figure 4, the user runs the application and chooses the service either Using GPS or CellID and clicks Submit. When the user clicks Submit application goes to background and listens for SMS. During the correct SMS arrival the application communicates with the Google map server and retrieves the needed information.

General Constraints

The primary constraint for the software is security. The password confirmation is considered as one security level to identify client with full access. The password confirmation decreases the risk of insecure use of the software other than the software owner.

Assumptions and dependencies

The main assumptions and dependencies are described as follows:

1. The application will be dependent on Google maps server. If the required service is not offered by the Google maps server, then the application will not give expected results.

2. GPS accuracy can be up to several meters depending on the device's GPS signal and connection. The device must support GPS and it should allow Google Maps access to it.

3. The device must support Cell-ID location and the accuracy depends on cell tower density and available data in Google's Cell-ID location database. Accuracy may be approximated at distances up to several thousand meters since coverage for Google's Cell-ID location databases varies by location and is not complete.

Usage Intensity

Usage Intensity means that how often the software will be used by the user. The expected usage for the software will be 24 hours a day, 7 days a week. This also depends on the user since the user can decide when to use it.

4.1.2 Hardware and Software Requirements

This section discusses hardware and software requirements and why Android was chosen to be used in the implementation of the application.

The Programming Language, Android was chosen to implement the project due to the following reasons.

1. No need for licensing, distribution, or development fees or release approval processes required.

2. GSM(Global system for mobile communications), EDGE (Enhanced Data rates for Global Evolution), and 3G(third generation) networks for telephony or data transfer, enables to receive SMS and enables to send and retrieve data across mobile networks

3. Provides Comprehensive APIs for location-based services such as GPS and Cell-ID.

4. Gives support for background processes like Service and BrodcastReceiver.

5. Gives full support for application that integrate and use Google's map service.

The Platform used was Google map APIs 2.1-update1 together with Eclipse 3.5 Galileo IDE. The choice of Eclipse 3.5 Galileo was recommended by Google for Android developers for this version of Android SDK.

The Hardware used was an Android device named HTC Hero brown. The device had Firmware version of Android 2.1-update and Browser version of webkit 3.1.The following figure 5 shows the software information.

Figure 5: Description of software information of the device used.

In figure 5 the Build number is an indicator of which numerical version of the current overall system was built by developers for the device.

4.1.3 Scenarios

User activities includes Running Application, Choosing service, Using GPS, and Using Cell-ID while receiving SMS and doing giving the expected service is for the application. The scenarios bellow briefly explains the user activity together with application responses.

Running Application is an activity happened when the user has the actor role in which the user clicks it and runs it. Table 4 summarizes this activity.

Table 4: Running Application Scenario

Name:	Running application
Summary:	No summery available at the moment
Actors:	The user
Frequency:	At any time
Preconditions:	•The user has active and valid access to the tracking application •has mobile phone compatible to the application •Knows how to use the Phone and the application and has the application installed
Descriptions:	The user selects the application and runs it
Post conditions:	No post conditions at the moment

As summarized in table 4, the user has to run the application to use the software. This is important since the application uses Internet and SMS service which are not free of charge.

Choosing Service is an activity in which the user selects either GPS or Cell-ID to retrieve location information. Table 5 summarizes this activity.

Table 5: Choosing Service user Scenario

Name:	Choosing Service
Summary:	No summery available at the moment
Actors:	The user
Frequency:	At any time
Preconditions:	The application is active
Descriptions:	User selects either use GPS or Use CellID
Post conditions:	No post conditions at the moment

As summarized in table 5, the user must select the service type in order to use it.

Using GPS is the activity where the user decides to use GPS as the location service provider. Table 6 summarizes this activity.

Table 6: Using GPS user Scenario

Name:	Using GPS
Summary:	No summery available at the moment
Actors:	User
Frequency:	At any time
Preconditions:	The application is active
Descriptions:	User selects Use GPS at this time application saves the state of service type
Post conditions:	No post conditions at the moment

In table 5 the user must choose Use GPS in order to retrieve the location of the target phone. At this point the application must save the state and remember which service to use.

Using Cell-ID is the activity where the user chooses Cell-Id for retrieving location information. Table 7 summarizes the activity.

Table 7: Using Cell-ID user Scenario

Name:	Using CellID
Summary:	No summery available at the moment
Actors:	The user
Frequency:	At any time
Preconditions:	The application is active
Descriptions:	The User selects Use CellID at this time application saves the sate of service type
Post conditions:	No post conditions at the moment

As summarized in table 7, the user must choose Cell-ID as location service provider and the application must save its state. During SMS arrival Cell-Id must be used by the application.

Submitting is the activity in which the user decides what to do with the software and sends it to background. The summary of the activity is shown in table 8.

Table 8: Submitting user Scenario

Name:	Choosing Service
Summary:	No summery available at the moment
Actors:	The user
Frequency:	At any time
Preconditions:	Application is active
Descriptions:	The User selects either use GPS or Use CellID and presses Submit
Post conditions:	No post conditions at the moment

Table 8 summarizes the last activity performed when the user plays actor role. The user must click Submit button for the application to go to background.

Receiving SMS is the final activity, and the actor in this case is the application itself. Table 9 summarizes the activity

Table 9: Application Receiving SMS Scenario

Name:	Choosing Service
Summary:	No summery available at the moment
Actors:	Application
Frequency:	At any time
Preconditions:	The application is active
Descriptions:	After the user selects either use GPS or Use CellID and presses submit, the application goes to background and initiates Service and Broadcast Receiver. At this point the application is listening for SMS arrival and If the request is to send location, it will send back location of the phone to be SMS that contains link to the map together with additional information including longitude and latitude, street address, post code, and region name of the target phone location.
Post conditions:	No post conditions at the moment

Even though it is not summarized in table 9, it is important to mention that the application needs special permission to receive and send SMS.

4.2 Implementing an Android Location Application

The application has one main activity class, one service class and one receiver class. The activity class named Soft2050.java defines the user interface and handles user interactions. The Soft2050.java has been defined as the default activity of Soft2050 inside AndroidManifest.xml file. In there, if the user chooses use Cell-ID or Use GPS then the class dispatches broadcast Intents events which are responsible for starting for listening SMS arrival. This is performed by receiver class named Soft2050Receiver.java. So during SMS arrival, if SMS body is "1234567", the application receiver class will start a service through the service class called Soft2050Service.java, and if the SMS body is "2345678", then the receiver class will make Use of Google's Cell-ID to retrieve location information. The service class is responsible for retrieving location information using GPS.

Implementing the activity class called Soft2050.java, which displays the User interface (UI) is shown in figure 6:

Figure 6: The User interface of Soft2050

The first point is to define the resource definition file for the UI. The file is buttons.xml file which is described below.

The first step followed was to define the layout structure and hold all the elements that appear to the user. The Layout is the architecture for the user interface in an Activity. [25; 26]

```
<?xml version="1.0" encoding="utf-8"?>
<LinearLayout
xmlns:android="http://schemas.android.com/apk/res/android"
android:layout_width="fill_parent"
```

```
android:layout_height="fill_parent">
</LinearLayout>
```

Another LinearLayout to hold the RadioGroup is created but this time height set to wrap_content. The RadioGroup will hold the two radio buttons. Grouping the two radio buttons inside the RadioGroup makes sure that checking one radio button that belongs to a radio group unchecks any previously checked radio button within the same group.

```
<LinearLayout
…
<LinearLayout
android:orientation="horizontal"
android:layout_width="fill_parent"
android:layout_height="wrap_content">
<RadioGroup
android:id="@+id/RadioGroup01"
android:layout_width="wrap_content"
android:layout_height="wrap_content"
<RadioButton
android:id="@+id/RadioButton01"
…
android:text="Use Gps"></RadioButton>
<RadioButton
android:id="@+id/RadioButton02"
…
android:text="Use Cellid"></RadioButton>
</RadioGroup>
```

Inside the very same LinearLayout tag, another Linearlayout, containing TextView and Button is created with the height and width being "wrap_content".

```
<LinearLayout
…
<TextView
android:id="@+id/TextView01"
android:text="Choose 1"
</TextView>
<Button
```

```
android:id="@+id/Button01"
…
android:text="Clear Choice"></Button>
</LinearLayout>
</LinearLayout>
…
```

Finally, Inside the Main LinearLayout another LinearLayout defining resource definition for another button with Text Submit is created.

```
<LinearLayout
  …
<LinearLayout
android:orientation="vertical"
…
android:gravity="bottom">
<Button
android:id="@+id/submit_demo"
…
android:text="Submit"
android:gravity="center" />
</LinearLayout>
</LinearLayout>
```

After defying the resource definition file, it is time to load buttons.xml in onCreate() method event handler of the activity class. This is done by using the setContentView() method. The code snippet below shows how it was done:

```
public class Soft2050 extends Activity {
…
@Override
public void onCreate(Bundle savedInstanceState) {
super.onCreate(savedInstanceState);
setContentView(R.layout.buttons);…}
```

Once loading the UI using the activity class, the UI must interact with the user, which is described below.

When the user clicks on the "submit" button, the application goes to background. This is done by calling Soft2050.this. moveTaskToBack(true) inside OnClick(), as shown below:

```
…
public void onClick(View v ){
Soft2050.this. moveTaskToBack(true);}});
 …
```

In the following it is described how the onCheckChanged() method has been implemented. The method uses instance of RadioButton to do the following.

If the user selects any of RadioButtons, first the method checks if the checkid is not equal to -1, to check if any RadioButton is currently checked, if true, the method creates instance of RadioButton and gets the text label of the RadioButton informing the user which of the RadioButtons the user has chosen.

```
…
TextView tv = (TextView) findViewById(R.id.TextView01);
if (checkedId != -1) {
RadioButtonrb = (RadioButton) findViewById(checkedId);
if (rb != null) {
tv.setText("You chose: " + rb.getText());}}
else{
tv.setText("Choose 1");}
…
```

If the user selects checked Id for Use CellID or Use GPS, the method creates instance of intent in which the intent dispatches a broadcast Intent through the class named Soft2050Receiver. This class is discussed in the implementation of the receiver class but the task of the class is to listen for SMS arrival.

```
…
if(checkedId == 1){
Intent intent = new Intent(Ctx,Soft2050Receiver.class);
Soft2050Receiver start = new Soft2050Receiver();
start.onReceive(Ctx, intent);}
```

```
else if(checkedId == 2){
Intent intent = new Intent(Ctx,Soft2050Receiver.class);
Soft2050Receiver start = new Soft2050Receiver();
start.onReceive(Ctx, intent);}}});
```

The implementation of the receiver class named Soft2050Receiver.java is described below.

This Class is responsible for receiving SMS, and to do this, the class has registered a BroadcastReceiver to listen to an Intent action associated with receiving an SMS.

```
…
<receiver android:name=".Soft2050Receiver" android:enabled="true">
<intent-filter>
<action android:name="android.provider.Telephony.SMS_RECEIVED" />
</intent-filter>
</receiver>…
```

The class should extend BroadcastReceiver (i.e base class code that will receive intents sent by sendBroadcast().).

```
public class Soft2050Receiver extends BroadcastReceiver
…
```

The class has private method implementation called getMessagesFromIntent(), taking an Intent as a parameter and returning the reference to one-dimensional array that contains the received message. First, a static reMsgs variable is declared and then set to null. Second, the message bundle is retrieved with a call to getExtras(). Third, with in the try-catch block, the bundle is checked if an array of objects contains a PDU-data (i.e. data format for wireless protocol.) and used the static variable retMsgs to retrieve the PDU data. Fourth, in the for loop the message was created with a call to SmsMessage.createFromPdu() from PDU data . It is good to have the try-catch. One reason could be the bundle might not contain any data.

```
…
private SmsMessage[] getMessagesFromIntent(Intent intent){
```

```
SmsMessage retMsgs[] = null;
Bundle data = intent.getExtras();
try{
Object pdus[] = (Object [])data.get("pdus");
retMsgs = new SmsMessage[pdus.length];
for(int n=0; n <pdus.length; n++){
byte[] byteData = (byte[])pdus[n];
retMsgs[n] = SmsMessage.createFromPdu(byteData);
}}
catch(Exception e)
{Log.e(Soft2050.Soft_debug_tag, "fail to create return message!", e);}
return retMsgs;}
```

Another important point is that the class overrides the onReceive() method. This method is to be called when BroadcastReceiver is receiving an Intent broadcast as show in Soft2050.java class implementation.

```
@Override
public void onReceive(Context context, Intent intent) {
…
```

Inside the onReceive(), the method checks if the received intent is the telephony's SMS received, and if not, it does nothing.

```
if(!intent.getAction().equals("android.provider.Telephony.SMS_RECEIVED
")) {return;}
```

If the above condition is true, the getMessagesFromIntent() will be called and the message will be retrieved to the variable msg. Inside the for loop, first, with a call to getDisplayMessage(), the message body is retrieved to the variable message. Second, within the if clause, the message has arrival checked, and received message checked if it matches the password constant defined in Soft2050Contants.java class (i.e. Soft2050Constants.PASSWORD = 1234567).Third, after checking the above condition, a new intent is created to start Soft2050Service. Then, using the putExtra() method, the phone number of the SMS sender was retrieved to be used by the Soft2050Service.java class. Forth, with a call to the context.startService() method, the service was started. The Soft2050Service class is responsible for retrieving the location of the device by using the deivce's GPS and Google maps.

```
...
SmsMessage msg[] = getMessagesFromIntent(intent);
for(int i=0; i <msg.length; i++){
String message = msg[i].getDisplayMessageBody();
if(message!=null&&message.length()>0
&&message.matches(Soft2050Constants.PASSWORD)){
Log.i(Soft2050.Soft_debug_tag,  message);
Intent mIntent = new Intent(context, Soft2050Service.class);
mIntent.putExtra("dest", msg[i].getOriginatingAddress());
context.startService(mIntent);
}...
```

In the above code, the else if clause checks if the message is not equal to null, and then checks if it matches it matches Soft2050Constants.PASSWORD2 (i.e. defined in Soft2050Constants.java class as 2345678). If the condition is true, the device's location will be retrieved by using Google's Cell-ID.

```
else if (message != null &&message.length() > 0
&&message.matches(Soft2050Constants.PASSWORD2))
{...
```

To obtain the Cell-ID of a device, the GsmCellLocation class was used. Below the first two lines show the declaration of the location and cellID and lac member variables respectively.

```
...
GsmCellLocation location;
intcellID, lac;
```

The next step is creating an instance of the TelephonyManager class. The TelephonyManager is used to obtain an instance of the GsmCellLocation class.

```
TelephonyManager tm=
(TelephonyManager)context.getSystemService(Context.TELEPHONY_SERVICE);
```

```
location = (GsmCellLocation) tm.getCellLocation();…
```

The next code snippet shows the GsmCellLocation class instance is used to obtain the device's cell ID and Location Area Code (LAC) by a call to its getCid() and getLac() methods respectively.

```
cellID = location.getCid();
lac = location.getLac();
…
```

However getting Cell-ID and LAC is not enough to get the location of the device. To get the location of the device, these two values have to be resolved into latitude and longitude. The following code shows how it is done.

First, an HTTP connection to the Google Maps API is opened.

```
…
String slocation = "";
try {
String urlString = "http://www.google.com/glm/mmap";
URL url = new URL(urlString);
URLConnection conn = url.openConnection();
HttpURLConnection httpConn = (HttpURLConnection) conn;
…
httpConn.connect();
```

Second, using the WriteData() method defined, a data containing cellID and lac values is posted to the Google Map API to retrieve the corresponding latitude and longitude values. Then the response is obtained by a call to the getInputStream() method.

```
…
OutputStream outputStream = httpConn.getOutputStream();
WriteData(outputStream, cellID, lac);
…
InputStream inputStream = httpConn.getInputStream();
DataInputStream dataInputStream = new DataInputStream(inputStream);
…
```

After getting the latitude and longitude values, the values concatenated together with a link to Google Map to the static string variable named slocation. This was done to get the corresponding Google Map link.

```
…
slocation += "\n" + String.format("http://maps.google.com/maps?q=%f",
lat) + "%20" + String.format("%f", lng) + "\n";
…
```

Third, the class Geocoder instance is being used to do reverse Geocoding, the process of transforming latitude and longitude values into an address. So, first, an instance of Geocoder class is constructed followed by addr variable.

```
Geocoder gc = new Geocoder(context, Locale.getDefault());
Address addr;
…
```

Fourth, inside the for loop, first by using the addr instance, a call to the togetLocality(), getThoroughfare(), getFeatureName(), getAdminArea(), getSubAdminArea(), and getPostalCode() was made. The above call will return thoroughfare, feature, administration, sub-administration names of the address, and postal code of the address respectively and it is important to note that some values cloud be null.

```
for(int j=0; j<myList.size(); j++){
addr = myList.get(i);
if(addr.getLocality()!= null )
slocation += addr.getLocality();
if(addr.getThoroughfare() != null )
slocation += "|" + addr.getThoroughfare();
if(addr.getFeatureName() != null )
slocation += "|" + addr.getFeatureName();
if(addr.getAdminArea() != null )
slocation += "|" + addr.getAdminArea();
if(addr.getSubAdminArea() != null )
slocation += "|" + addr.getSubAdminArea();
if(addr.getPostalCode() != null )
slocation += "|" + addr.getPostalCode();}}…
```

Finally, by getting an instance of an SMSManager using a call to the getDefault() method, the Soft2050 application was able to send the retrieved location information. After this a call to the sendTextMessage() made with parameters slocation (i.e. the String variable containing the location information) and phone number of the SMS sender.

```
SmsManager sms = SmsManager.getDefault();
…
sms.sendTextMessage(msg[i].getOriginatingAddress(),  null,  slocation,
null, null);}}}}
```

For the class to be able to send an SMS, access device location, and use the Internet, the class needs to add permissions in the manifest file as follows:

```
…
<uses-permission android:name="android.permission.SEND_SMS" />
<uses-permission
android:name="android.permission.ACCESS_COARSE_LOCATION" />
<uses-permission android:name="android.permission.INTERNET" />
…
```

The implementation of the Service class named Soft2050Service.java is described as below.

As stated above, in the implementation of Soft2050Receiver, the receiver class makes use of the service class, when the users request to locate their device by GPS. Simply calling the startService() method will do. In this project, it was important to recall that inside the onReceive() method of the Soft2050Reciver class, for received message types which matches "1234567", the startService() method was called. Calling the startService() method from another class, will result in the corresponding call to the onStart() method of the service class. The service class must override the onStart.

This class must add a service block containing the Soft2050Service class inside it, extend the Service class and override the onCreate(), onStart(), and onDestroy() methods, as shown below:

…

```
<service android:name=".Soft2050Service"></service>
…
public class Soft2050Service extends Service {
private NotificationManager NM = null;
LocationManager locationManager = null;
…

@Override
public IBinder onBind(Intent arg0) {
return null;}

@Override
public void onCreate() {
NM = (NotificationManager)getSystemService(NOTIFICATION_SERVICE);
locationManager=
(LocationManager)getSystemService(Context.LOCATION_SERVICE); }
```

The service class makes use of the method getGPSStatus() which returns the name of the GPS provider if any. First, the allowed Location Providers String will contain any allowed location provider, if null should be initialized. Second, it returns LocationManager.GPS_PROVIDER which is name of GPS provider if any.

```
private Boolean getGPSStatus(){
String allowedLocationProviders =
Settings.System.getString(getContentResolver(),
Settings.System.LOCATION_PROVIDERS_ALLOWED);
if (allowedLocationProviders == null) {
allowedLocationProviders = "";}
return
allowedLocationProviders.contains(LocationManager.GPS_PROVIDER)}
```

The class has overridden the onStart() method. As discussed in the beginning of this section, the method should be called to start the service of this class. The call is not direct. Instead a call to Context.startService() will result in a call to the onCreate() method, then finally followed by a call to onStart() method.

```
public void onStart(final Intent intent, intstartId) {
super.onStart(intent, startId);
```

…

The Soft2050 should provide implementation of LocationListener. The object of LocationListener consists of four methods; two tell the application if the provider has been disabled or enabled, one tells the status of the provider, and the last one location information. In this project the application was implemented only using the onLocationChanged() method.

```
LocationListener locationListener = new LocationListener() {
…
```

Implementation of onLocationChanged() method, the method receives Location object with most recent location information.

```
public void onLocationChanged(Location location) {
```

The class uses an SmsManager instance to send the recent location information. Inside the sendTextMessage method, a call to intent.getExtracts() gets the originating SMS sender phone number from the Soft2050Reciver class. The getAddr() method which is described below, will take in location instance and from there will get latitude and longitude and will do reverse Geocoding which was described earlier in receiver class implementation section. Finally, the call to the removeUpdates() will remove current registration for location update.

```
SmsManager.getDefault().sendTextMessage(intent.getExtras().getString("
dest"),null,getAddr(location,getApplicationContext()),deEvent,
deEvent);
locationManager.removeUpdates(this);}…}};
```

The class checks for location update using the LocationListener instance. Second, the class creates instance of Location and uses it to get the last known location of the device using GPS by calling getLastKnownLocation("gps"). Third, if the GPS location result is not found, the Location instance is used to get the last known location using another network provider by calling getLastKnownLocation("network"). Finally, PendingIntent instance is created and used to send Broadcast with a call to the getBroadcast() method.

```
locationManager.requestLocationUpdates(LocationManager.GPS_PROVIDER,0,
0, locationListener);
Location location = locationManager.getLastKnownLocation("gps");
if (location == null)
location = locationManager.getLastKnownLocation("network");
if (location != null){
PendingIntent
deEvent=PendingIntent.getBroadcast(this,0,new Intent("IGNORE"), 0);
…
```

In order to send the required location information, first, with a call to .getExtras(), the String variable dest will retrieve the destination phone number from Soft2050Receiver class. Second, with a call to getAddr() method the String variable sms will retrieve the reverse Geocoding result of the method. Finally, onStart() method uses SmsManger.getdefault to send an SMS to the specified destination with location information of the target phone.

```
…
String dest = intent.getExtras().getString("dest");
String sms = getAddr(location, this);
SmsManager.getDefault().sendTextMessage(dest,null,sms,deEvent,deEvent)
;}}…
```

Finally, for the service class, permissions have to be added inside the Android manifest. This is because the application needs permission to use location permission.

```
…
<uses-permission
android:name="android.permission.ACCESS_FINE_LOCATION" />
```

4.3 Testing and Signing

Testing

In this project, the black box testing system was chosen to run the test. The application Soft2050 testing included UI and functionality testing.

User Interface testing was started by running the application, after running the application, the UI which is defined in the requirement specifications of the project was displayed. In order to run the Software on the device, the following procedure was followed:

1. Inside the Manifest file the Debuggable attribute was set to true.
2. The HTC hero device was connected to the computer via USB.
3. Soft2050 < Run As < the device was selected and double clicked.

In order to see the application logcat file, the Dalvik Debug Monitor was started by executing the "ddms" command inside tool folder of the Android SDK as follows:

1. C:\Program Files\Android\android-sdk-windows\tools\> ddms.

The expected UI was displayed, similar to that of figure 6. It has the two radio buttons and the other buttons which were expected to show. UI functionality tests namely "Use Gps", "Use cellid", "Clear choice", and "Submit" were run. The results were obtained as shown in figures 7, 8, and 9.

Figure 7: User selected "Use Gps"

Figure 8: User Selected "Use Cellid"

Figure 9: User Pressed "Clear Choice" Button.

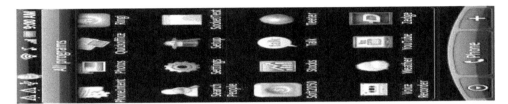

Figure 10: User pressed "Submit" and application goes to background.

The result of the UI functionality test proved that UI reacts to user interactions successfully. A summary of the UI functionality test is shown in table 10.

Table 10: User interface test for Soft2050

Test Case	Expected Result	Result(true/false)	Evidence
User Selected"Use Gps" Radio button.	Selected mode on "Use Gps" radio button and "Choos 1" of button "Clear Choice"should changed to "You Choosed: Use Gps"	True	Figure 7
User Selected "UseCellid" Radio button.	Selected mode on "Use Cellid" radio button and "Choos 1" of button "Clear Choice" should changed to "You Choosed: Use Cellid"	True	Figure 8
User pressed Clear Chice	If there is any Radio button is in Selected mode, It should change to now selected mode.	True	Figure 9 Note: User has already pressed the button at this moment.
User pressed "Submit"	Application should go to background and should be on All programs window.	True	Figure 10.

It is important to consider figure 10 which shows the program windows. The program windows were visible after the user pressed the Submit button on the software.

Functionality Test

In this project, the purpose of the functionality test was to test if the software could perform as the user expected. The selected locations for running the test were Avaruuskatu 3, 02210 Espoo and Biskopsbron 11, 02230.The different test cases made are described in the following.

1. The user selected "Use Cellid" and pressed "Submit"

Here the GPS status was considered when running the test. This is to check if the user experience that using GPS while disabled will give only the last known location. The following sub test cases namely "Phone in dual network mode and GPS disabled" and "Phone in dual mode GPS enabled" were carried out.

a) Phone was in the dual network mode and the GPS was disabled.
The user sent an SMS with the message body "2345678". The result is shown below in the figure 11, for Avaruuskatu 3, and figure 12 for Biskopsbron 11.

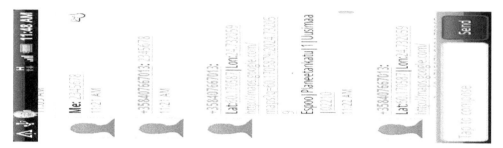

Figure 11: User selected "Use Cellid" and phone dual mode.

Figure 12: User selected "Use Cellid" and phone dual mode.

b) Phone was in dual mode and GPS was enabled.

The user sent an SMS with message body "2345678". The result was the same as case (a) for both locations, which is shown in figures 11 and 12.

2. The user Selected "Use Gps" and Pressed "Submit"

This test was carried out by moving from one location to another location. This done to make sure that the location information updates when moving from one location to another. The following sub test cases namely "Phone in dual network mode and GPS enabled" and "Phone in dual mode GPS disabled" were carried out.

a) Phone was in dual network mode and GPS was enabled.

The user sent an SMS with the message body "1234567". The result is shown in figures 13 and 14. The test was made both inside the building and outside the building but no difference could be seen at the moment of the test.

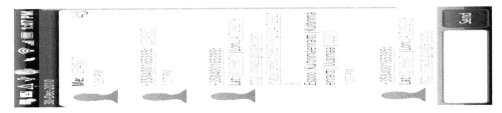

Figure 13: User selected "Use GPS" and GPS was enabled.

Figure 14: User selected "Use GPS" and GPS was enabled.

b) Phone was in dual mode and GPS was disabled

This test case was executed first in Avaruuskatu 3 and then after moving to the second test location Biskopsbron 11. So at the second location, the device's GPS was disabled. The user sent an SMS with the message body "1234567". The result is shown in figure 14. It is the last known location.

Signing

Now that the application is functioning as expected, it is time to sign it. The Android system requires that all installed applications to be digitally signed with a certificate whose private key is held by the application's developer. [19]

Since the application is ready for end-users, it is time to sign the application with a release mode. In order to do this, it must be signed with a suitable private key. The following steps are taken to do so:

1. The first step is to generate a private key by executing a keytool command inside the Java Development Kit's (JDK) bin directory, as show in figure 15.

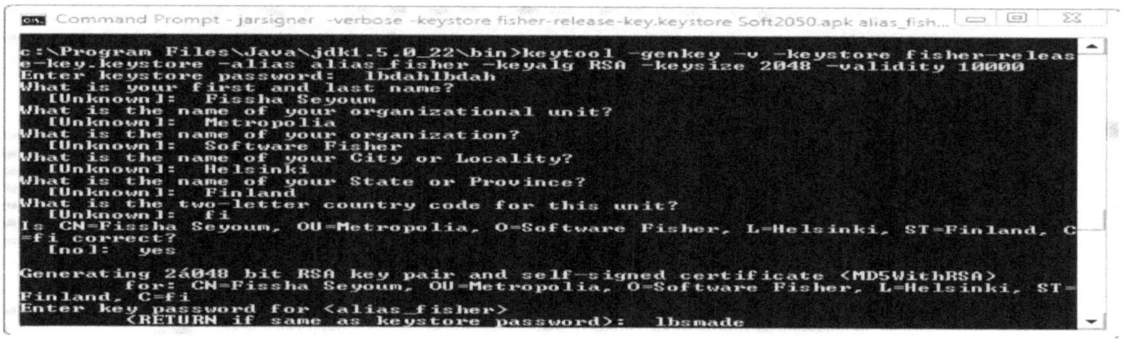

Figure 15: Executing the Keytool command that generates a private key.

2. The last step is to sign the Soft2050.apk file by executing the jarsigner command and then verifying if it is signed correctly by executing the jarsigner –verify command as shown in figure 16.

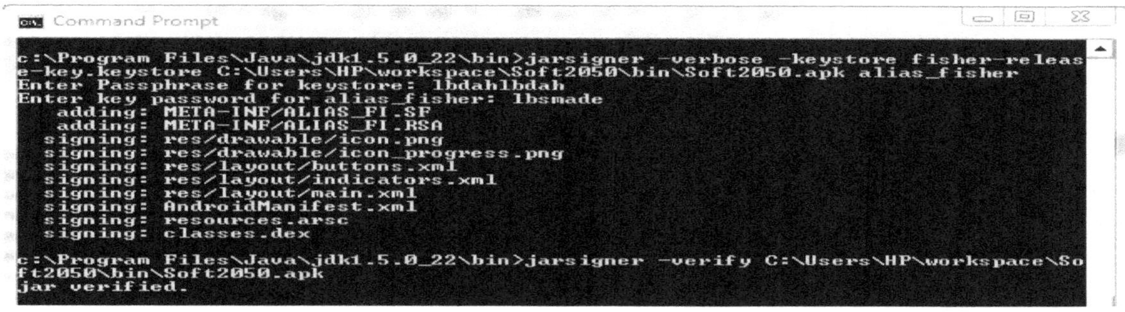

Figure 16: Executing Jarsigner to sign Soft2050 package.

5 Discussion

The application Soft2050 was fully developed fulfilling the requirement specifications set at the beginning of this project. The application can send back location information as seen in the figures 11, 12, 13 and 14.

It has been noticed from the figures that the actual locations of the test places were some 100 meters away. As seen from figures 11 and 12, test case 1 when the user selected "Use Cellid" and pressed "Submit", the location information was not exact. When checking on the Google map, the retrieved location Planeetankatu 1 was serveral 100 meters away from test place 1 Avaruuskatu 3. The second result for the second test place (i.e Länsiväylä) was even worse while the real location was Biskopsbron 11. This problem in accuracy of location information was because the coverage for Google's cell ID databases varies by location and is not complete. As seen for Avaruuskatu 3 the corresponding retrieved location was better than the second test location Biskopsbron 11.

The second test case, when GPS was enabled on the device, the retrieved location information was better. For the first test location Avaruuskatu 3 the retrieved location was Kuitinmäenraitti, Espoo which was very near to Avaruuskatu 3. When considering the second test location, the retrieved location information was Biskopsbron 8, Ussimaa the result was checked on Google map and it was almost exact. When considering Biskopsbron 11 case the result was better than that of Avaruuskatu 3. This was because GPS accuracy can be up to several meters depending on the device's GPS signal and connection.

As mentioned in sub test case (b) of 2, the test case where the device's GPS was disabled was executed first in Avruuskatu 3 and after that in the second test location, which was Biskopsbron 11. The result was Biskospsbron 8 which was the last known location. The result was as expected.

5.1 Benefits

As discussed above, the Soft2050 has benefits when using both Cell-ID and GPS as the location retriever.

The advantages of using the Cell-ID over the GPS could be that, first, the user of Soft2050 will get approximated location information in many places and second, the user will not care if the GPS is enabled or disabled or the device could not have GPS at all. Finally, while using GPS and since GPS has to be enabled all the time, the device will consume battery faster.

There are advantages of using GPS over Cell-ID. First, the user of Soft2050 will get almost exact information on the location of the device. Second, in some devices, the manufacturer may not have enabled API to allow for Cell-ID and therefore not all devices support Cell-ID.

5.2 Drawbacks

Based on the testing and the discussion above, using Soft2050 has drawbacks. In many cases, the user of Soft2050 may suffer from high phone bills. This is because when using GPS, every time the Soft2050Service class makes an update, it sends an SMS and uses mobile network to download the link. The other problem is the user does not get exact location in many cases.

It is important to consider battery consumption since mobile phones have limited power source. As a result the user of the software should consider high battery consumption while using GPS. Finally, the user should be aware of getting empty messages from the software. This is caused when there is no Cell-ID database coverage in the area.

5.3 Future Development

The software needs to be further developed. In other words, it will include a number of functionalities. There are users who would like to have this application as a background invisible application. As a result, the application will run in the background, which means there will be an option for the user to run the application in the background, so that the target phone user will not have any idea if the application exists or not. It is not enough that the application runs in the background to be invisible. This is to consider while sending an SMS request to the target. The target phone user will not see the SMS notification for the secret SMS to be sent. This can be done by adding a silent SMS functionality. The other important feature the application will have is SMS copying. SMS copying means that the application will send copy of sent or received messages from the target phone to the owner of the software at request. Furthermore, the application will add a spy call functionality which will be used to listen to a conversation between the target phone and any other call receiver or caller.

6 Conclusions

The goal of this project was to develop a mobile phone tracking application for Google Android phones. The application was expected to include the use of GPS and Cell-ID to track the location of the mobile phone. The tracking software named Soft2050 was fully developed using Android.

During testing it was found out that it was possible to retrieve a location both by GPS and Cell-ID while using Google Android. This was possible because Android gave support for the background processes such as service and broadcast receiver. Using the receiver, it was possible to listen to an SMS arrival and launch a service.

The development process was fast. This was possible for a number of reasons. First, Android provided APIs for location-based services such as GPS and Cell-ID. Second, having Eclipse with Application Development Kit Plug-in as a choice to develop the application led to an easy means of debugging and testing. Especially the use of Dalvik Debug Monitor Server was the reason for an efficient device testing.

This type of application could be categorized as spying software. However, the tracking application was found important since it will allow users to trace lost phones or to locate lost people. The application can be developed further by adding a number of features such as running in the background, SMS copying and making a spy call. It is recommended to avoid the misuse of such software.

References

1   Spy Mobile Phone [online], Mobile Spy; 21 January 1999
         URL: http://www.spy-mobile-phone.com
         Accessed: 12 March 2010

2   iPhone Spy Software [online], Applicationle iPhone Spy Software; 13
         January 2010
         URL: http://www.iphone-spy-software.com.
         Accessed: 15 March 2010

3   FlexiSpy [online], FlexiySpy Software features; 13 January 2006
         URL: http://www.flexispy.com/spyphone-features-compare.htm#special.
         Accessed: 15 March 2010

4   What is NeoCall? [online], NeoCall; 31 August 2006
         URL: http://www.neo-call.com/en/price_features.php
         Accessed: 8 October 2010

5   Nokia spy software [online], NokiaSpyPhone; 12 August 2007
         URL: http://www.nokiaspyphones.com/comparespyphones.html
         Accessed: 11 October 2010

6   Ultimate Mobile Spy [online], E-stleath; 11 December 2008
         URL: http://www.e-stealth.com/Listening-Devices_c_582.html
         Accessed: 1 November 2010

7   Mobile Spy Tool [online], F-Secure; 31 August 2006
         URL: http://www.f-secure.com/weblog/archives/00000962.html
         Accessed: 19 March 2010

8   Mobile Security 6 [online], F-secure; 19 January 2010
        URL:http://www.fsecure.com/system/fsgalleries/datasheets/
        FSC_ms6_usa.pdf
        Accessed: 20 March 2010

9   KasperSkyMobile Security [online], KasperSky; 23 June 1997
        URL: http://usa.kaspersky.com/products-services/
        -home-computer-security/mobile-security
        Accessed: 3 November 2010

10   BullGuard Internet Security [online], BullGaurd; 22 February 2001
        URL: http://www.bullguard.com/bullguard-security-center.aspx
        Accessed: 2 November 2010

11   What is Android? [online], Android Developers; 16 April 2007
        URL: http://developer.android.com/guide/basics/what-is-android.html
        Accessed: 22 March 2010

12   Jerome, Dimarzio. Android a Programmer's Guide. United States of
        America: McGraw-Hill Companies; 2008

13   FAQ [online], Open Handset Alliance; 5 November 2007
        URL: http://www.openhandsetalliance.com/oha_faq.html
        Accessed: 23 March 2010

14   Android timeline [online], Android Academy; 4 October 2007
        URL: http://www.androidacademy.com/4-android-timeline
        Accessed: 8 November 2010

15   Android Market [online], Android Feeder; 16 December 2007
        URL: http://androidfeeder.com/
        Accessed: 10 November 2010

16 Paid Application Availability [online], Android Market; 16 April 2007
URL: http://market.android.com/support/bin/answer.py?hl
=en&answer=143779
Accessed: 11 November 2010

17 Application Developer not happy with Android [online], GigaOM; 4August
2008
URL:
http://gigaom.com/2009/11/29/android-application-developers-not-
happy/
Accessed: 12 November 2010

18 Sale with Google Checkout [online], Google Checkout; 16 December 2007
URL: http://checkout.google.com/seller/sales.html
Accessed: 12 November 2010

19 Signing Application [online], Android Developers; 16 December 2007
URL:
http://developer.android.com/guide/publishing/application-signing.html
Accessed: 12 November 2010

20 Shane Conder and Lauren Darcey. Android Wireless Application
Development.
United States of America: Addison Wesley; 2010

21 The Truth about Mobile Application Stores [online], Read Write Web;
20 April 2003
URL:http://www.readwriteweb.com/archives/the_truth_about
_mobile_Application_stores.php
Accessed: 30 04 2010

22 Mark L. Murphy Beginning Android.
United States of America: Apress; 2009.

23   What is the Android NDK? [online], Android Developers; 16 April 2007
        URL: http://developer.android.com/sdk/ndk/index.html
        Accessed: 01 05 2010

24   Dalvik [online],Android Open Source Project; 5 November 2007
        URL: http://source.android.com/porting/dalvik.html
        Accessed: 10 05 2010

25   Ed Burnette Hello, Android.
        United States of America: The Pragmatic Bookshelf; 2008.

26   Rick Rogers, John Lombardo, Zigurd Mednieks, and Blake Meike. Android
        Application Development.
        United States of America: O'REILLY: 2009.

27   Retro Meier. Professional Android Application Development.
        United States of America: WILEY: 2009.

28   Android is now available as open source [online], Android Open Source
        Project; 16 April 2007
        URL: http://source.android.com/posts/opensource
        Accessed: 17 05 2010

29   Timeline of Androids evolution [online], Android Academy
        Project; 20 May 2008
        URL: http://www.androidacademy.com/4-android-timeline
        Accessed: 19 01 2011

30   Android Architecture [online], Android Developers
        Project; 16 April 2007
        URL: http://developer.android.com/guide/basics/what-is-android.html
        Accessed: 20 05 2010

31   Android 2.2 Platform highlights [online], Android Developers
        Project; 16 April 2007
        URL: http://developer.android.com/sdk/android-2.2-highlights.html
        Accessed: 19 05 2010

32   Free VS Paid Applications comparison [online], Read Write Web
        Project; 14 May 2003
        URL:
        http://www.readwriteweb.com/archives/the_truth_about_mobile_Applicat
        ion_stores.php
        Accessed: 21 06 2010

YOUR KNOWLEDGE HAS VALUE

- We will publish your bachelor's and master's thesis, essays and papers

- Your own eBook and book - sold worldwide in all relevant shops

- Earn money with each sale

Upload your text at www.GRIN.com
and publish for free